101 Coolest Things Do in New Zealand

© 2016 101 Coolest Things

All rights reserved. No part of this publication may be reproduced, distributed, or transmitted in any form or by any means, including photocopying, recording, or other electronic or mechanical methods, without the prior written permission of the publisher, except in the case of brief quotations embodied in critical reviews and certain other noncommercial uses permitted by copyright law.

Introduction

So you're going to New Zealand, huh? You lucky lucky thing! You are sure in for a treat because New Zealand is truly one of the most magical countries on this planet. There's a mix of incredible landscapes, thrilling adventure activities, world-class festivals, and delicious food and drink that makes New Zealand one of the most enduringly popular tourist destinations on the face of the earth.

In this guide, we'll be giving you the low down on:
- the very best things to shove in your pie hole, whether that's copious amount of wine from the classic wine trail, or crayfish fresh from the ocean
- the best shopping so that you can take a little piece of New Zealand back home with you, whether that's from a local flea market or a glass blowing studio
- incredible festivals, whether you want to party all night in the mountains, or you'd prefer to chow down at an oysters festival
- the most thrilling outdoor activities, such as white water rafting on a raging river or snowboarding in the mountains
- the coolest historical and cultural sights that you simply cannot afford to miss like a Maori buried village and contemporary art galleries in Auckland

- where to party like someone from New Zealand and get down with the locals
- and tonnes more coolness besides!

Let's not waste any more time – here are the 101 coolest things not to miss in New Zealand!

1. Go White Water Rafting on the Waikato River

If you are something of an adventurer, you are going to fall head over heels with New Zealand. The extreme landscapes make it the perfect place for lovers of adventure sports, and it doesn't get much more adventurous than powering along the rapids of a forceful river current. The Waikato River is the longest river in the whole country, and you can find rapids that are both tranquil and very strong, so no matter your experience or rafting ability, there's an adventure waiting to be had.

2. Enjoy a Maori Hangi Feast in Rotorua

New Zealand is a country with impressive history, culture, and gastronomy, and by indulging in a Hangi feast, you can explore all of these facets of the country, because this is a traditional feast that extends back for thousands of years in the Maori culture. The Hangi method of cooking is below the ground with hot rocks, and ingredients typically include chicken, beef, potatoes, and pumpkin. Because Rotorua still has a strong connection to Maori culture, it's a good place to experience one of these feasts.

3. Find Treasures at Otara Flea Market

Once you have seen all the sights and visited as many museums as you can muster, it's time to take it easy with a little bit of relaxed shopping, and there is no better place for that than at the Otara Flea Market in Auckland. The market is only open on Saturday mornings so you'll have to make sure you don't have a big Friday night out if you want to make the most of the experience. With more than 150 vendors, it's the largest street market in New Zealand.

4. Unwind at Wairakei Terraces and Thermal Health Spa

The landscapes of New Zealand are nothing short of gorgeous. But when you are in this country, you not only have the opportunity to look at the vistas from afar, you can actually immerse yourself in the nature and have a wonderfully relaxing experience. At the Wairakei Terraces you can find cascading silica terraces that flow into geothermally heated pools. You can also have massage and beauty treatments there, making it the ideal place for an incredibly indulgent experience.

5. Hike Up Ben Lomond Mountain

If you like to get active and enjoy the landscape by immersing yourself in activities on holiday, you've chosen an awesome holiday destination in New Zealand, and a hike up Ben Lomond mountain is sure to get you more than a little bit breathy. The hike to the top can be done in 4-6 hours, which is certainly a challenge, but means that you can be back in Queenstown by night time. The trek zig zags and is rocky in places, but the reward of the view from the top is more than worth the slog.

6. Walk Through New Zealand's Oldest Prison

New Zealand is a country full of attractions, and while you might not plan on visiting the old prisons of the country, Napier prison might just twist your arm. The prison was first put to use in the 1860s and was a functional prison all the way up until the 1990s. Now you are invited to take a tour around the prison, where you will see the hanging yard, the conditions that prisoners used to live in, and you can even have your mugshot taken. Smile for the camera!

7. Watch Chocolatiers at Work at the Silky Oak Chocolate Company

If you consider yourself something of a chocaholic, you might want to take a day off from the usual sightseeing and adventure activities, and head to the Silky Oak Chocolate Company. There is a museum where you can learn about the history of chocolate, but the highlight is, of course, the chocolate shop, where you can actually watch the chocolatiers hard at work, and sample some of the deliciousness that is produced there every day.

8. Indulge at the Bluff Oyster Festival

If you have a taste for decadence, you no doubt love any opportunity to slurp down a few juicy oysters. Well, you need to trust us when we tell you that you haven't tasted oysters at their best until you have tried them from New Zealand. The best place to try a whole bunch is at the Bluff Oyster Festival, which takes place every March in Bluff. There are fun activities like the oyster opening competition, but the highlight is, of course, savouring the taste of all the locally caught oysters.

9. Have a Ski Trip on Mt Ruapehu

New Zealand has such a breadth of landscapes that you can enjoy sunny beach days as much as adventurous ski trips. If you are the adventurous sort and you are visiting in the winter months, a ski trip on Mount Ruapehu is a must. This mountain is, in fact, an active volcano, but that doesn't stop coach loads of tourists visiting to enjoy the snow each year. There are beginner to advanced ski fields so you and your friends and family can join in with the fun, no matter your experience or ability.

10. Take the New Zealand Classic Wine Trail

It is no secret that New Zealand is pretty much heaven on earth for wine lovers, and one absolute must for wine aficionados in New Zealand is a trip across the classic wine trail. This wine trail covers three regions of the country – Hawke's Bay, Wairapara, and Marlborough – meaning that you get to taste a lot of great wine and explore different parts of New Zealand at the same time. You can drive yourself through the regions, and you can even cycle depending on your fitness levels and how tipsy you intend to get.

11. Enjoy the Colours of Hastings Blossom Festival

New Zealand is a country with epic nature and landscapes, but if you want to experience some of the colours of nature in a city setting, you can't beat the Hastings Blossom

Festivals, which takes place every September as a way to celebrate the onset of spring in Hawke's Bay. On the weekend, you will see more than fifty floats, all covered in flowers, being paraded along the streets.

12. Cycle with Takaro Trails

Are you the person who likes to get active on holiday? If so, you have absolutely chosen the best holiday destination. One adventure that you shouldn't miss is the chance to hit the pedals of a bike with Takaro Trails. Takaro Trails is a tour company that specialises in cycling adventures for all abilities around Hawke's Bay. Whether you just want to hire a bike and find your own way around or you want to join in an organised mountain biking adventure, they will have something for you.

13. Learn About Honey at Arataki Honey

Who doesn't love a delicious slick of honey on toast? Well, if you want to take your honey appreciation to the next level, you should know about Arataki Honey, which is one of the largest beekeeping enterprises in the southern hemisphere. At their visitor centre, you can discover the history of the brand, you can learn the whole process of how bees make honey, and, of course, you'll have plenty of opportunity to try yummy honey as well.

14. Party at the Incredible WOMAD Festival

WOMAD, standing for World of Music, Arts, and Dance, is one of the best loved and most established arts festivals on the planet. The festival pops up all over the world, and each year you can find it in New Plymouth in New Zealand. The party takes place every March, and it's the best place to see artistic talent from all over the world. In previous years, acts that have performed at WOMAD New Zealand include De La Soul from the USA, Songhoy Blues from Mali, and DakhaBrakha from Ukraine.

15. Feel the Country's History at Te Papa

Te Papa is the official museum and gallery of New Zealand, and if you want to get to grips with both the history and culture of the country, this is the place to get your education. The name loosely translates as "the place of treasures of this land", and that couldn't be any more accurate. Once inside, you will find a herbarium with a quarter of a million dried specimen, ancient fossils, incredible art works, and a wonderful library.

16. Stroll Through Christchurch's Botanic Gardens

The Christchurch Botanic Gardens are some of the most beautiful botanic gardens to be found anywhere in New Zealand. They date all the way back to 1863 and cover a space of more than 21 hectares. In the gardens, you can find a water garden with irises and lilies, an Asian rock garden, a rose garden with more than 250 rose species, a herb garden, a conservatory complex with cacti, and lots more besides.

17. Camp Overnight at Anchorage Beach

As a series of islands, New Zealand has some seriously great coastline, and one of our favourite beaches in the country has to be Anchorage Beach. You can find sloping golden sand backed by a forest, and it's the perfect place to spend a relaxed weekend. But if you really want to have the wild New Zealand experience, make sure that you check in with the conservation campsite by the beach so that you can camp under the stars and watch the sun rise over the ocean.

18. Take in a Movie at the New Zealand International Film Festival

With all of the incredible landscapes to explore and adventure activities to enjoy in New Zealand, it's understandable that you might want to kick back and relax with a good movie at the end of your vacation. Well, if you're a real cinema buff, you can do one better by attending the New Zealand International Film Festival, which is hosted across various cities, including Wellington and Auckland. The festival brings the best of world cinema to New Zealand, while also promoting local talent.

19. Take in the View from Sky Tower in Auckland

When you are in Auckland, you are likely to spot one building looming over the horizon at all times – the Sky Tower. The Sky Tower stands tall at 328 metres, which makes it the tallest structure in the southern hemisphere, and scaling the building gives you the perfect opportunity to take in all the majesty of the city. On Level 51, you can view the city from the observation deck, and on Level 52, you can take in the view from a revolving restaurant.

20. Get Back to Nature at Kiwi Birdlife Park

New Zealand is a nature lover's paradise, and it is home to a hugely diverse range of wildlife. You can explore some of this wildlife on a trip to Kiwi Birdlife Park in Queenstown, which is specifically dedicated to the conservation of reptiles and birds. Inside this park is one of the only places where you will get to see the rare and nocturnal Kiwi bird – the bird that New Zealand natives are named after. You can also enjoy audio tours, conservation shows, and Kiwi feeding sessions.

21. Enjoy an Indulgent Meal at Meredith's Restaurant

New Zealand may not be the cheapest country in the world, but even so, there are days when you should let the budget slide and indulge. If you only have one chance to eat a fancy meal in Auckland, make sure that it's at Meredith's. The restaurant prides itself on its use of local ingredients, but everything is given a twist. Take the chorizo broth or black pudding puree, for example. To fully appreciate the culinary craft of the restaurant, treat yourself to the eight course tasting menu.

22. Hike Through the Franz Josef Glacier

New Zealand is a country with so many different kinds of landscapes. You'll find white sand beaches, volcanic craters, rolling hills full of greenery, and even glaciers. The Franz Josef Glacier is a 12 kilometre long glacier on the south island that is explored by a quarter of a million tourists every year. It's possible to take guided treks through the ice, and also to take helicopter rides above the glacier to take in all the grandeur of this unique natural formation.

23. Go Fly Fishing in the Tongariro River

If your idea of a perfect afternoon is sitting beside a riverbed with a fishing rod in your hand, there are numerous places where you can enjoy great fly fishing in New Zealand, but we think the best of them all has to be the Tongariro River. The great thing about the Tongariro River is that there is no defined fishing season, and you can attract plump trout all year round. Perfect for a delicious fish supper.

24. Down a Few Bottles at Little Beer Quarter

While New Zealand is a country that is better known for its wines than its beers, if you are a beer lover you don't have to miss out. At least not if you head for the Little Beer Quarter in Wellington. With twelve beers on tap and more than one hundred types of bottled beer, it's the place for all beer lovers to geek out. You'll also be able to find local beers produced in New Zealand if you want to try something brand new.

25. Have a Thrilling Luge Experience in Rotorua

The Rotorua area is a place where you can enjoy both culture and adventure. If you fancy having an adrenaline pumping afternoon, it doesn't get more thrilling than speeding down on a luge track. At the Skyline Luge in Rotorua, you will be strapped into a luge vehicle at the top of Mount Ngongotaha, and sent whizzing down one of three winding tracks.

26. Hang With Wellington's Hipsters in Laundry

If you find yourself in Wellington on a Friday night with nothing to do and a desire to party, you can find the trendsters of the city in a building called Laundry. From the outside, it looks like a regular laundry place, but poke your head in and you'll find a small but uber-cool bar full of Wellington's twenty-somethings. And if you're not a night owl, you can still experience the charm of the place as it served up a killer brunch at a reasonable price in the daytime.

27. Chow Down at the Marlborough Wine & Food Festival

If you are a wine lover, it probably hasn't escaped you that New Zealand is one of the most prolific countries in the world when it comes to wine, and you can experience its incredible wine culture at the Marlborough Wine & Food Festival, which is hosted every year in February in a picturesque vineyard. You'll get to experience tasting tutorials from the region's leading winemakers, and there will also be culinary events so you won't go hungry either.

28. Discover Sea Life at the National Aquarium

As a set of islands, New Zealand is surrounded by lots of water and lots of sea life. If you don't fancy taking to the open waters but want to discover the country's marine life in more comfortable surroundings, a trip to the National Aquarium in Napier is a very good idea. At the Napier Aquarium, you'll find water dragons, sea horses, a waterfall area, New Zealand geckos, sea turtles, and more besides. It makes a really fun day out for the whole family.

29. Discover NZ Arts & Crafts at Vesta

Shopping for souvenirs to take back home can be stressful when you are only confronted with tacky t-shirts and branded mugs, and that's why you should bypass the tourist shops and head for Vesta, a design store on the edge of Queenstown Lake. The store is located inside the oldest house in Queenstown, a small cottage that dates back to 1864. Inside, you'll find all kinds of creative goodies made by NZ locals, such as ceramics, glassware, and original textiles.

30. Party Hard at Soundscape

While New Zealand is best known for its incredible landscapes and natural beauty, if you are a party person, you'll definitely find some places to let your hair down in the country. For our money, there's no better party than Soundscape, a street festival that takes place during March and July in the city of Hamilton. Each time, a part of Alexandra Street is closed off so there is space for music stages and lots of dancing, and the parties always continue into the night at the local clubs.

31. Try Strange Foods at Wildfoods Festival

When visiting a new place for the first time, you should always try to eat as much local food as you possibly can, but at the annual Hokitika Wildfoods Festival, which takes place every March, you might get more than you had bargained for. At this festival, the order of the day is anything that comes from Mother Earth, and you could find yourself chowing down on treats such as earthworms, snails, sheep's brains, lambs' testicles, and more besides.

32. Watch Kapa Haka, a Traditional Maori Performance

If you want to get to grips with the traditional Maori culture on your trip to New Zealand, you need to know about Kapa Haka, which is the authentic kind of Maori performance involving a compelling combination of dancing, chanting, and song. There are different kinds of dances, and while some will be graceful and romantic, others will be ferocious, using war weaponry. Rotorua is a place that is alive with Maori culture and a good place to catch one of these performances.

33. Listen to a Choir Sing in the Waitomo Glowworms Cave

If you want to treat yourself to a truly magical experience on your trip to New Zealand, how does navigating into a cave that lights up with glow worms sound? Well, this species is found exclusively in New Zealand, so it's really is a one of a kind experience. But wait, you can make the experience even more magical by visiting the cave when the cave's very own choir performs there. The dimensions of the cave and the quality of the rock give the space incredible acoustics.

34. Watch Wellington Light Up at Wellington LUX

Wellington is a beautiful city at any time of year, but if you want to see Wellington when it transforms into a positively magical urban space, you should consider timing your trip so that it coincides with Wellington LUX, which is held at the end of August each year. Across five days, the whole city is illuminated with an incredible array of light installations that are projected on to buildings, public spaces, and even the river.

35. Sail Through Lake Taupo

While there are many adventure activities that you can do in New Zealand, such as white water rafting or tobogganing, sometimes you might want to enjoy the natural landscape in a more restful way. If that sounds good to you, a day of sailing on Lake Taupo will be right up your street. There are quite a few sailing companies that can take you on trips so that you don't have to do anything but relax and take in the views from the deck.

36. Celebrate Matariki in Wellington

Something really unique about being in New Zealand is that you get to learn about and experience some of the ancient Maori culture, which for many people is still a strong part of the national identity. Matariki is an important celebration that marks the start of the Maori New Year in June, and one of the biggest celebrations is in Wellington. The festivities include the sighting of a seven star constellation, lots of arts, dance, and music events, and storytelling events from the local Maori communities.

37. Eat Fresh Crayfish From Nin's Bin

Since New Zealand is totally surrounded by water, you can expect to eat some pretty spectacular seafood on your visit. If you'd rather forego the fancy restaurants and want to eat where the locals eat, you can't do much better than Nin's Bin, which is essentially a ramshackle shack on the edge of the coast at a beautiful beach called Half Moon Bay. It is the place to buy the freshest crayfish caught directly from the sea.

38. Sink a Few Beers at Beervana

While New Zealand is famed for its wine production, if you're a beer lover there is no need to fear, particularly if you plan to visit Beervana in Wellington, which as the name would suggest, is a beer lover's paradise. The event takes place over two days in August in Wellington Stadium, and guests at the festival will be treated to beers from more than 45 breweries all around New Zealand. There will be tasting sessions, food and beer pairings, and you can purchase lots to take home.

39. Eat Lots of Deliciousness at Whitianga Scallop Festival

One of the greatest things about New Zealand is all the delicious seafood that is available to eat right throughout the country. You'll discover this first hand if you etch a trip to the Whitianga Scallop Festival into your New Zealand itinerary. It takes place every September on the south island, and visitors to the festival can indulge at more than 60 food and wine stalls, take part in scallop shucking competitions, and be entertained by live music as well.

40. Get Artsy on the Oakura Arts Trail

New Zealand might be better known for its incredible landscapes than its vibrant arts culture, but if you are an arts lover, we don't think you'll be disappointed on your trip, particularly if you choose to go on the Oakura Arts Trail. This event takes place across a few weekends in October and November, and throughout these weekends, local practicing artists open up their studios to the public so that you can see the process and the stories behind the work. It's a great way to talk to the artists, get a feel for the local scene, and maybe even purchase something special.

41. Take a Scenic Walk Along the Huka Falls Walkway

Huka Falls, a set of waterfalls along the Waikato River are the most visited natural attraction in New Zealand, and it's with good reason. The falls are spectacular, and they are also easy to reach if you take the Huka Falls Walkway. This walkway extends for 6km, and you'll get to walk along the beautiful

Waikato River before being confronted with some of the most stunning waterfalls on the planet. The walk is fairly easy and suitable for families.

42. Feel Local History at the New Zealand Maori Arts & Crafts Institute

Maori culture extends back for thousands of years, and while you might not see many signs of this ancient culture in the houses of ordinary New Zealanders, you can get a great feel for it at the New Zealand Maori Arts & Crafts Institute in Rotorua. The institute plays an active role in keeping the Maori arts alive, and when you are inside, you can see original carvings, beautiful weavings, as well as drawings and paintings.

43. Indulge a Sweet Tooth at the New Zealand Chocolate Festival

If you fancy forsaking a day or hiking or mountain climbing for something a little more indulgent, you can't get much more indulgent than the New Zealand Chocolate Festival. This festival is hosted annually in Wellington, in the middle of August. At the festival, your chocolate appreciation will be taken to the next level. Master chocolatiers will make grand sculptures out of chocolate, they will create different kinds of cuisines from chocolate, and best of all, you'll get to sample plenty of the good stuff.

44. Relax With an Indulgent Mud Bath Spa

One of the greatest things about going on holiday is taking the time to relax, unwind, and push the stresses of everyday life to the very back of your mind. There are plenty of natural vistas that instantly inspire tranquillity in New Zealand, but if you want to seriously unwind, we recommend a trip to Hell's Gate, which is far more peaceful than it sounds. It is actually a geothermal spa in the Rotorua area, and the mud there is so nutrient rich that you can enjoy a mud spa and replenish tired skin.

45. Have Lots of Fun at the Big Gay Out

New Zealand is a very progressive country when it comes to its political attitudes, and this is reflected in the great freedoms that LGBT people have had in the country for many years. Same sex marriage has been allowed since 2013, and the community is protected by an array of anti-discrimination laws. The Big Gay Out is a major celebration of everything LGBT, and it happens every year in February. It's a time to wave a rainbow flag with pride and celebrate with the LGBT community in the street.

46. Cool Down With a Hokey Pokey

For lovers of sunshine, the summer months are definitely the best time to be in New Zealand. The colours of the landscapes are incredible, and strolls along the beautiful beaches are mesmerising. If you need something to cool you down on those warm summer days, a hokey pokey is what you need to try. This scrumptious dessert is essentially silky smooth vanilla ice cream with crushed pieces of honeycomb, and we guarantee that you'll be returning for a second scoop.

47. Take in the Wings Over Wairarapa Air Show

If you are a geek for planes, you need to know all about the Wings Over Wairarapa air show, which is renowned for its incredible flying programme, and takes place every two years in either January or February. Make your way to Wairarapa during the festivities and you will be treated to incredible aerobatic displays, the chance to get up close to real aircraft from WWI and WWII, and there will also be plenty to eat and drink on the ground.

48. Walk Through the Treetops in Redwoods

For nature lovers who love to see trees and greenery all around them, there aren't many places more magical than the Redwood Grove in New Zealand, a forest full of tall trees, native plants, and even lakes. But if you want to experience the forest in a different way, you can actually traverse the terrain through the treetops via a selection of suspension bridges hoisted in the air. This might not be one for people with vertigo, but otherwise, it will be an experience you'll always remember.

49. Explore a Piece of Cinema History

The Lord of the Rings and The Hobbit films are some of the most successful and most loved films ever made. On your trip to New Zealand, you can actually visit the transformed sheep farms that were transformed into the land of the Shire for the movies. The set is a true work of art with many details such as fake moss around the Hobbit Holes. The tour guides will take you through the whole set and describe where each part of the set is used in the movies.

50. Visit New Zealand's Oldest Winery, Mission Estate

New Zealand is a country that is sure to be on the radar of all wine lovers. While in the country, it's a great idea to visit the wineries and vineyards, and one that is more special than most is the Mission Estate, located in Hawke's Bay. The reason it's so special is that it's the country's oldest winery, established in 1851. There is an elegant restaurant on site, and there are even rooms if you fancy spending the night.

51. Take Surfing Lessons at Raglan

With so much coastline, New Zealand provides ample opportunity for watersports enthusiasts to have the time of their lives. If a spot of surfing takes your fancy, there are a few great spots around the coast, but we are particularly fond of the town of Raglan, located on the west coast of the north island. The waves there can reach spectacular heights, but don't fear if you're a total beginner, there are a few surf schools in the town that can ease you into the waves until you gain your confidence in the ocean.

52. Hang Out at Auckland Indie Market

The Auckland Indie Market is just about the coolest place to be in the whole city, and even if you don't particularly enjoy shopping there will be something for you to enjoy. At the market, you'll find hand crafted items, lots of edgy design work, and more. But beyond what's on sale, you'll find live bands and buskers, a huge selection of food trucks that will satisfy even the pickiest of palettes, and art exhibitions as well.

53. Cruise the Waters of Milford Sound

Milford Sound is one of the most iconic spots in New Zealand, and it's with good reason. This fjord on the south island was famously called the eighth wonder of the world by Rudyard Kipling, and the best way to take in all of its sensational beauty and grandeur is with a cruise along its waters. On a cruise, you'll see incredible rock formations, seals basking on the rocks, waterfalls cascading from the mountains, and vast expanses of serene water.

54. Take a Burger Pilgrimage to Fergburger

Okay, you probably haven't travelled all the way to New Zealand to eat burgers, but let's face it, sometimes nothing else will do than a big, fat, juicy burger. And if the burger pangs strike, the place to be is Fergburger in Queenstown. Sometimes the queue is round the block, but believe us when we say that it's worth the wait. There are more than 30 types of burger on the menu including a venison burger, falafel burger, and lamb burger.

55. Bungee Jump Over the Nevis River

If you are a true adrenaline junkie, white water rafting and snowboarding might not be adventurous enough for you? Well, how does a bungee jump over one of the country's rivers sound? Well, it starts to get even more hair raising when you consider that this is the country's highest bungee at a height of 134 metres. You will experience eight and a half seconds of terrifying freefall before springing back up. Would you dare?

56. Feel the Beat at St Jerome's Laneway Festival

St Jerome's Laneway Festival, otherwise simply known as Laneway, is one of the best music events on the New Zealand calendar. The street music festival originated in Australia, but now takes over the streets of Auckland every February. The atmosphere is relaxed, everybody wants to have a good time, and the music talent is exceptional. Acts that have performed in previous years include Belle & Sebastian, FKA Twigs, and Jessie Ware.

57. Watch a Show at the St James Theatre

If you find yourself in Auckland, and you want to do something more with your evening than going to the pub, the St James Theatre is both an entertaining and cultural option. This theatre opened in the 1920s, and was originally created as a stage for vaudeville performances. It is the place in Auckland to catch classical performances such as an opera show or a ballet performance, which also makes it the perfect excuse for dressing up and having a fancy night.

58. Check Out a Frisbee Golf Course in Queenstown

For adventure travellers, there is no better destination in New Zealand than Queenstown. There is bungee jumping, skydiving, and more besides. But if you fancy a quieter day in the city, we heartily recommend a fun game of frisbee golf. Frisbee golf is similar to regular golf except that, you guessed it, a frisbee is involved rather than a golf ball. Work your way around the course, and try to get the frisbees into the holes.

59. Look at an Art Deco Masterpiece, the Daily Telegraph Building

If you are a fan of architecture, New Zealand probably isn't the first country that would come to mind, but amongst all of that nature, there are some buildings that are nothing short of jaw dropping. Napier is a city that is full of art deco buildings, and one of our favourites has to be the Daily Telegraph Building. Built in the 1930s, it is full of wonderful zig-zag shapes, and looks like it should be part of the New York art deco scene.

60. Find Something Special at a Queenstown Market

If you are something of a shopaholic, you are bound to be taken by the vibrant market culture that exists all over New Zealand. One of our favourite markets is the Queenstown Market, which is a place where you can discover local arts and crafts, and take something really special back home with you. The founders are committed to supporting the works of local artists on the south island, and you can find anything from jewellery to glassware, ceramics to original textiles.

61. Boost Your Health at the Wellbeing Fair

One of the loveliest things about taking a trip away is that you can get some perspective on your life, relax, unwind, and recharge your batteries. The beauty of New Zealand is a huge wellness booster as it is, but if you really want to dedicate some time to wellness on your trip, you can visit the monthly Wellbeing Fair in Auckland too. There is always organic food and drinks, pamper treatments, yoga sessions, health talks, and more.

62. Fish For Your Own Prawns

Once you taste the seafood in New Zealand, seafood back home will never be the same again. And one place where you can have more of an interactive experience with your dinner is at Huka Prawn Farm, which just lies a little outside of Taupo. This farm produces a staggering thirty tonnes of prawns each and every year. If you decide to visit, you'll be given the chance to fish for your own prawn supper, or you can simply enjoy a prawn based meal in their on-site restaurant.

63. Ride the Skyline Gondola of Queenstown

If you're in Queenstown and want to know the best place for a killer view, the good news is that no hiking or climbing is involved. Instead, you can simply jump aboard the Skyline Gondola, and the views from your cabin will be unparalleled. Once at the top, there are plenty of activities to enjoy as you'll find a luge and go kart centre. Or if you just want to take it easy, dine at the restaurant on top of the mountain.

64. Get Artsy at the Auckland Arts Festival

If you are an arts lover and you love nothing more than exploring the local arts scene on vacation, you might be more drawn to well established arts cities like Paris and Florence, but you absolutely should not discount Auckland, particularly during the Auckland Arts Festival. It is the premiere arts festival in New Zealand, and it showcases art exhibitions, theatre performances, dance shows, circus shows, multimedia art, and more. It takes place every March.

65. Hike to Volcanic Craters in Tongariro National Park

Tongariro is the oldest national park in New Zealand, and it has been recognised by UNESCO as one of the 28 mixed cultural and natural heritage sites. There are so many things to absorb your attention within the park, but one of the most fun things has to be a hike across the Tongariro Alpine Crossing, which will take you on an unforgettable journey to volcanic craters, lava flows, and emerald coloured lakes.

66. Check Out the Glass Sculptures at Lava Glass

Before you leave New Zealand, you will surely want to purchase some items that will always remind you of your stay in this stunning country. Trust us when we tell you to bypass the souvenir shops, and head straight to Lava Glass, an artisanal store in the Lake Taupo area. This glass blowing studio is somewhere that you can grab something really unique. And even if you don't end up buying something, a stroll around their glass sculpture garden is a very pleasant way to pass a free hour.

67. Chow Down for Auckland Restaurant Month

We have to eat food every day, so we might as well make the food we put into our mouths count for something, right? Well, foodies from around the world need to know about Auckland Restaurant Month, when you'll have a food experience in New Zealand like no other. There are all kinds of events during the month such as street food markets, a pop-up farmers' market, special tastings with restaurants in the city, and wine tastings as well.

68. Catch a Rugby Match at Eden Park

If you're a sporty kind of person, there is only one sport that you need to know about when in New Zealand, and that's rugby. The population is positively fanatical about this sport, and never is that more evident than when you are actually on the sidelines of a rugby match, cheering on the players. So what could be better than going to see a match in the national stadium, Eden Park? Tickets are sought after so be sure to book well in advance.

69. Tour the Wellington Chocolate Factory

If you are a chocaholic, and who isn't, you should definitely etch some time into your schedule to tour the Wellington Chocolate Factory. This is the only chocolate factory in New Zealand that is open to the public, and a visit will deepen your appreciation of the magic substance. You'll learn exactly how the beans are sourced and where they come from, then how the staff at the factory treat the beans, and eventually transform them into silky chocolate bars.

70. Have a Sky Diving Adventure

There's certainly no shortage of hair raising adventures for thrill seekers in New Zealand, and perhaps the most thrilling of them all is a sky diving experience. Sky diving is basically jumping out of an airplane, and freefalling before opening your parachute. It's all the more incredible if the landscape beneath you offers something for the eyes, and a popular place for sky dives in New Zealand is in Wanaka.

71. Visit the Buried Village in Rotorua

If you want to get to grips with the history of New Zealand, but you aren't so keen on museum hopping, the Buried Village in Rotorua is a place where the country's history really comes to life. The village was created as a Maori settlement in 1848, but in 1886 a volcano erupted and the whole village was submerged under lava. You can now visit and look at the excavated ruins of the village as well as some old relics that have been recovered.

72. Enjoy a Picnic by Whangarei Falls

There is nothing quite as enjoyable as spending time in nature and whiling away a few relaxed hours by a cascading waterfall. One of our favourite waterfalls in the country is Whangarei Falls, a classic curtain waterfall with water that rushes down for 26 metres. The bottom of the waterfalls are safe for swimming, and there are picnic spots around the falls where you can have a relaxed afternoon with loved ones.

73. Brave the Heights of the Auckland Sky Walk

If you fancy yourself as something of a daredevil, you don't need to go white water rafting or scuba diving – you can actually have an adventure right in the heart of Auckland city. The Auckland Sky Tower is a huge building that dominates the city skyline, but instead of just taking in the view, you can also walk on top of the building. You will be strapped in, and then you will walk around a narrow walkway around the edge of the building at a height of 192 metres.

74. Tuck Into Fish & Chips From Greenwoods Fresh Catch

When you are by the ocean (and you are never far away from the sea in New Zealand), there is nothing quite like enjoying a traditional fish and chips summer. There are plenty of fish and chips restaurants over the country, but our choice is Greenwoods Fresh Catch in Auckland. This place has won numerous awards and they cook something simple the way that it should be. Soft fish, crisp batter, and chunky chips.

75. Be Wowed by Maori Rock Carvings at Taupo

If you want to get to grips with the ancient Maori culture of New Zealand, Lake Taupo is definitely a place where you should spend some time. Inside the Mine Bay, you'll find some beautiful, ten metre high carvings that are only accessible by boat. Full disclosure – these were actually created in the 70s as re-imaginings of what the ancient carvings looked like, but they are still pretty spectacular, and well worth the journey.

76. Indulge an Inner Bibliophile at the Auckland Writers Festival

If your idea of a great time is having your head stuck inside a book, you may want to take a couple of days off from New Zealand's adventure activities, and head to the Auckland Writers' Festival, which is hosted every May. Bibliophiles will be in sheer heaven, as there will be readings from world renowned and local authors, workshops in writing and publishing, book signings, super interesting panel discussions, and more book related fun.

77. Sip on Beers in the Smash Palace Beer Garden

On a sunny summer day, there is nothing quite as enjoyable as relaxing in the outdoors with a cold glass of beer. If that sounds good to you, the Smash Palace Beer Garden in picturesque Christchurch will be right up your street. But this is no ordinary beer garden. You will find a psychedelic school bus, ramshackle furniture, and other hipster elements combined with a rose garden and edible herb patch.

78. See Penguins at the International Antarctic Centre

While in the city of Christchurch, it's absolutely imperative that you take the time to visit the International Antarctic Centre. Antarctica is not a place that many people get to visit, but you can be wowed by it in Christchurch. Highlights include a cave with an Antarctic storm, an ice plunge challenge, and more. But the highlights for every visitor are always the adorable penguins, which will never fail to put a smile on your face.

79. Explore Arts & Crafts at the Titirangi Village Market

At the centre of Titirangi culture, you can find the Titirangi Village Market, which is held on the last Sunday of every month. Each time, you'll find more than 130 stallholders selling original arts and crafts from the area. You will also be entertained by live music throughout the day, and you'll have the chance to sample homemade dishes and organic coffee.

80. Take the Scenic TranzAlpine Train

In New Zealand, taking the train is not just a way of getting from one place to another but an attraction in its own right, particularly if you take the opportunity to board the TranzAlpine line. You will start your journey in Christchurch and end up in Greymouth on the south island. Throughout your journey, you will encounter the Canterbury Plains, you'll motor alongside the beautiful Waimakiriri River, and you'll even traverse the heights of the Southern Alps.

81. Learn About Cheese Making in Kaikoura

There are so many sheep and cows all over New Zealand that it should come as no surprise that there is a huge cheese culture in the country, even though New Zealand cheese may not be internationally recognised. If you're a cheese lover, we recommend a trip to Kaikoura. In Kaikoura, you can actually visit the local factory where cheese is produced and learn about the process. And, of course, you'll have the chance to sample lots of delicious cheese too.

82. Get Tipsy at the Hokonui Moonshiners Festival

The Hokonui Hills is a part of New Zealand that is not famous for its natural beauty (although it is very beautiful there) but for the illicit production and trade of a home grown whisky or moonshine. Today, that culture is celebrated annually at the Hokonui Moonshiners Festival, which takes place every year at the end of March. You can expect live music, lots of dancing, and, of course, plenty of whisky drinking.

83. Take in a Concert at Auckland Town Hall

Although New Zealand is a country that is well known for its landscapes and natural vistas, there are times when you might want to dress up and do something in the evening time, and we can't think of anything better than taking in a show at the beautiful Auckland Town Hall. The building is more than one hundred years old and was built in the Italian Renaissance Revival Style. The town hall's organ is the largest musical instrument in the country, and if you have the chance to catch a recital here, grab it with both hands.

84. Have a Day of Learning at the Canterbury Museum

The Canterbury Museum in Christchurch is, without a doubt, one of the more impressive museums in New Zealand. Located in a gorgeous Gothic Revival building that dates back to the 1880s, the museum has a collection of rare Maori artefacts that tell the fascinating story of the country's history. There are actually more than 2 million items in the museum, including household tools, decorative objects, and art works.

85. Tour a Kiwi Orchard

If you could associate one type of food with New Zealand, what would that be? Possibly the kiwi fruit, right? As well as tasting lots of kiwis on your trip, you should also take the time to visit Kiwi360, which is a whole kiwi fruit visitors' centre with an orchard. On your trip, you can tour the grounds, find out how kiwi fruits are grown, and take home some kiwi related products from the kiwi shop.

86. Learn About Wearable Art in New Zealand

Okay, so you probably aren't heading to New Zealand to expand your knowledge of wearable art, but if you find yourself in Nelson with some free time, the World of Wearable Art museum is a great place to learn about something right at the cutting edge. Walk through the museum, and you'll find more than sixty wearable art garments, many of which are award winning creations imported from around the globe.

87. Take in All of Wellington From Mt Victoria Lookout

Wellington is definitely a beautiful city, but you can only appreciate the beauty of the city so much when you see it from the ground. But if you want to take in the whole vista of the city, you need to scale to the lookout point of Mt Victoria Lookout. It sits at a height of 196 metres, but you don't have to walk all the way up as the No. 20 bus will take you most of the way. From the top, you can see Tinakori Hill, the Hutt Valley, and the Eastern Harbour Bays.

88. Get to Grips With New Zealand's Maritime Heritage

Since New Zealand is a country that is totally surrounded by water, it should come as no surprise that the country has a very impressive maritime history, and it's something that you can learn all about at the New Zealand Maritime Museum in Auckland. The museum takes you on a journey across a huge expanse of time, right from the first Polynesian explorers. Inside, you'll be wowed by exhibitions on Maori vessels, maritime arts and crafts, whaling and sealing, coastguard services, port history, and lots more.

89. Ride in a Hot Air Balloon Over Waikato

The Waikato area on the north island contains lots of natural beauty, but look to the skies in March, and you'll see something other than clouds and stars. This is when the area is taken over by Balloons over Waikato, a 5 day festival that sees hot air balloons from all over the world taking to the skies. This is a beautiful sight in itself, but you can do one better and also book your own hot air balloon ride. From the air you'll see the Waikato river and the surrounding countryside.

90. Learn About the Kauri Tree at the Kauri Museum

Tucked away in a village called Matakohe, the Kauri Museum is one of the best kept secrets in New Zealand. The focal point of the museum is the magnificent Kauri Tree, and how the tree has supported the people of New Zealand since European settlers arrived in the country. It has the largest collection of kauri gum in the world, a huge selection of kauri furniture, and an extensive collection photographs and memorabilia from the kauri tree's long past.

91. Party in the Mountains at Rhythm & Alps

If you are a party person who also wants to experience the beautiful outdoor vistas of New Zealand, you don't have to compromise between the two if you choose to party at Rhythm & Alps, an annual festival that takes place every New Year's Eve in Wanaka. The basic but very brilliant idea is that you camp out in the stunning mountains of New Zealand with other people who like to party as much as you do, and you listen to awesome bands and dance until the sun comes up over the New Year.

92. Take a Scenic Flight Over Lake Tekapo

There are a number of beautiful lakes across New Zealand, but there is none more picturesque than Lake Tekapo on the south island. In fact, this lake is so beautiful that it is best appreciated from a great height, and the best way to take in all of its majesty is with a helicopter ride over the water. Yes, this is indulgent, but it's totally worth it. On your flight, you will get to take in vast swathes of blue water, nearby glaciers, and rocky mountain landscapes.

93. Feel the Expanse of the 90 Mile Beach

If you are a beach lover, you might be immediately darn to destinations like Thailand or Hawaii, but trust us when we say that New Zealand has more than its fair share of beautiful beaches, and the 90 mile beach is the most expansive of the lot. When you arrive on the beach, it seems like there is almost endless space for laying down your towel and catching a few rays, and if you fancy some beach time that's more adventurous, you can try out body boarding on the dunes just inland from the beach.

94. Have an Artsy Day at the Auckland Art Gallery

While you might not instantly think of Auckland as one of the major arts cities on the planet, once you have spent the afternoon wondering around Auckland Art Gallery you might just change your mind. This gallery opened in 1887, and it has the most extensive collection of local and international art in the whole country. It's a joy to discover New Zealanders such as Gretchen Albrecht, Marti Friedlander, and Frances Hodgkins in the collection.

95. Have a Magical Experience at a Blue Penguin Colony

In Oamaru on the south island, there is something very special – a colony of little blue penguins. Every evening, these penguins wade to the shore and head for their nests on the waterfront. There are stands set up on the coastline so you can see all of the action without actually disturbing the penguins in their natural habitat. Seeing penguins in a zoo is one thing, but seeing them go about their daily business in their natural surroundings is something altogether more magical.

96. Experience a Taste of Japan in NZ

Although they are on the same side of the world, Japan and New Zealand are separated by a vast swathe of ocean. Fortunately, you don't have to book an expensive flight to Japan to find Japanese culture in New Zealand, you just have to visit the Japan Festival of Wellington, which is hosted every couple of years. Throughout the festival you can learn Japanese calligraphy, you'll be introduced to a traditional tea ceremony, you can watch a taiko drumming show, and you can eat lots of delicious Japanese food.

97. Pick Your Own Berries in Nelson

On a summer day, there is little more appealing than walking around the countryside and picking your own fruit. Tamsan Bay Berries is a pick-your-own place out in sunny Nelson, ere visitors are welcome to pick their own raspberries, berries, and blackberries. You can then chow down on all the delicious fruit that you picked, and perhaps enjoy them with a creamy ice cream, which you can buy in the on-site café.

98. Have a Whale Watching Adventure at Kaikoura

New Zealand is totally surrounded by ocean, and that means that it's also surrounded by sea life. If you want to have an adventure on the open seas that you will never forget, it doesn't get much more mesmerising than whale watching. The best place for this is Kaikoura. You will be taken out on a boat where you will be able to spot magnificent sperm whales, as well as other marine life such as dolphins and seals.

99. Watch the Sunset at Raumati Beach

When you are in New Zealand, there are plenty of opportunities to get "off the beaten track" and simply bask in the country's natural beauty with nobody else around. Raumati Beach is probably somewhere you haven't heard of, but once you visit, it will be etched into your memory forever. There is nothing but golden sand, ocean, and a few fishermen – and that's the beauty of it. It's a particularly spectacular place for taking in a pink sunset.

100. Spend the Night in a Former Jail

When in New Zealand, you are likely to spend your nights in hotels and guesthouses, but if you fancy an accommodation option that is a bit different, you could spend the night in a former jail. Addington Jail, which is now simply called Jailhouse Accommodation, dates all the way back to 1874, but for the last 15 years or so, it's been a place where people want to have a unique accommodation experience. The owners actually play on the fact that it was a prison, and so you can expect some prison cell décor in your room.

101. Take Part in Napier's Art Deco Festival

For fans of beautiful architecture, there is one city in New Zealand that is absolutely unmissable. Not Wellington, not Auckland, but Napier. It's a great idea to stroll around the city and look at the architecture at any time of the year, but you can fully appreciate the Art Deco culture of the city during the Art Deco Festival which is held every February. Events included guided walks, prohibition parties, and Gatsby themed picnics.

Before You Go…

Thanks for reading **101 Coolest Things to Do in New Zealand**. We hope that it makes your trip a memorable one!

If you enjoyed this book, we would really appreciate it if you could take the time to leave a review over on the book's Amazon page.

Keep your eyes peeled on **www.101coolestthings.com**, and have a great trip!

Team 101 Coolest Things

Printed in Germany
by Amazon Distribution
GmbH, Leipzig